W9-BWG-312

THE INVENTION OF THE
COTTON GIN

BY NIKOLE BROOKS BETHEA

Published by The Child's World®
1980 Lookout Drive • Mankato, MN 56003-1705
800-599-READ • www.childsworld.com

Photographs ©: Library of Congress, cover, 1; William Hoogland/Library of Congress, 6; Shutterstock Images, 8; Everett Historical/Shutterstock Images, 9, 16, 23, 24; Percy Moran/Library of Congress, 10; SuperStock/Glow Images, 12; Glasshouse Images/Newscom, 14; Department of State/U.S. National Archives and Records Administration, 18; George N. Barnard/Library of Congress, 20; Ann Ronan Picture Library Heritage Images/Newscom, 22; Currier & Ives/Library of Congress, 26; Morphart Creation/Shutterstock Images, 28

ISBN 9781503816428
LCCN 2016945599

Printed in the United States of America
PA02321

ABOUT THE AUTHOR
Nikole Brooks Bethea is a licensed professional engineer. She earned a bachelor's and master's degree in environmental engineering from the University of Florida and worked as a professional engineer for 15 years. Most of Mrs. Bethea's publications are science and engineering books for children.

TABLE OF CONTENTS

FAST FACTS

- Inventor: Eli Whitney
- Date: Whitney received a **patent** for the cotton gin on March 14, 1794.
- Purpose: The gin sped up the process of removing the seeds from the cotton.
- Location: Savannah, Georgia, and New Haven, Connecticut.
- Special features: Eli Whitney's cotton gin consisted of five parts. They included the frame, the wooden cylinder covered with iron teeth, a slotted grating, a brushlike **clearer**, and the **hopper**.
- Impact: The cotton crop became so important in the south that it was called King Cotton.

TIMELINE

December 8, 1765: Eli Whitney is born.

Fall 1792: Whitney earns his degree at Yale College.

Winter 1792: Whitney begins his design of the cotton gin.

May 27, 1793: Whitney and Phineas Miller sign an agreement to share any profits from the patent of the cotton gin.

June 20, 1793: Whitney applies for a patent for his cotton gin.

October 15, 1793: Whitney mails a description and drawings to Thomas Jefferson for a patent.

March 14, 1794: Whitney receives a patent for his cotton gin.

May 11, 1794: Whitney delivers his first shipment of cotton gins to Miller.

June 21, 1794: Whitney and Miller form a business partnership. They operate as Miller & Whitney.

January 8, 1825: Whitney dies at age 59.

Chapter 1

WHITNEY'S IDEA

Eli Whitney couldn't stop thinking about it. Farmers needed a way to separate the green seeds from cotton. The year was 1792. Whitney was spending a few days on the Greene family's Mulberry Grove **Plantation** near Savannah, Georgia. Whitney was 26 years old. He had just finished college in Connecticut, and he was on his way to South Carolina. A teaching position awaited him there.

At the plantation, Whitney overheard people talking about the seed problem. Areas such as Georgia grew short-staple cotton. It had sticky green seeds. Removing these seeds from the white, fluffy cotton was time-consuming. The green seeds were much harder to remove than the black seeds in long-staple cotton. But long-staple cotton grew only in certain areas. Cottonseed was separated from fiber by hand. It could take hours to clean the seeds from one pound of cotton. A machine that could separate green seeds from cotton would make cotton farming more profitable.

Whitney thought about the problem. He knew he had the mechanical ability to find a solution. After all, he had grown up using tools in his father's workshop. He had learned to make wheels and chairs at an early age. He fondly recalled making a violin when he was about 12 years old. This led him to begin earning money by repairing violins.

Whitney smiled as he remembered faking a sickness one Sunday morning. This allowed him to skip church. He had wanted to take apart his father's watch. He wanted to see how it worked. But his father wouldn't allow it. As soon as his family left for church, young Eli started removing the pieces.

▲ Cotton was an important crop in the southern United States.

He was amazed to observe the movement in the watch. He realized how much trouble he would be in if he didn't get the watch back together. Piece by piece, he rebuilt the watch. Luckily, his father never noticed he had taken it apart.

Plantation owners forced slaves to do many jobs, such as ▶ packing cotton into bags.

Whitney also remembered the time when one of his stepmother's favorite knives broke. He proudly made a new knife that was almost exactly like the old one. The only difference was the stamp on it. He could have made that too if the tools hadn't been so expensive.

Whitney was always looking for ways to make money. Back when he was a teenager during the American Revolution (1775–1783), nails had been in high demand. They sold for a high price. Most were handmade. Whitney had created a machine to **manufacture** nails. By the end of the war, manufacturing nails wasn't profitable. So he looked for other business opportunities. He noticed fashion was becoming more important in society. Therefore, he began making pins for ladies' hats. Next he took on the task of making walking canes.

In his mid-20s, Whitney finished at Yale College. That meant he now had debts to repay. He was on the lookout for another business opportunity. His teaching job would pay a decent salary. But during his stay on the Greene family's plantation, Whitney thought about other ways to make money. He was sure he would make a fortune if he could find a way to separate the seeds from short-staple cotton.

◀ **The American Revolution, led by George Washington, lasted for more than eight years.**

11

Chapter 2

DEVELOPING THE COTTON GIN

Whitney soon learned that the teaching position in South Carolina paid only half of what he had been promised. He turned down the job. Whitney wondered what he was going to do next. He was out of money and far from home. The Greenes were some of his only friends in the South.

Catherine Greene was the widow of Nathanael Greene. He had been a major general in the Revolutionary War. Phineas Miller, also a graduate of Yale College, managed the Greenes' plantation.

Whitney had an interest in studying law. Mrs. Greene said he could stay at her home and begin his studies. Whitney was very thankful. But he couldn't stop thinking about the problem with cleaning green seeds from cotton. Whitney decided to put his studies on hold.

The Greene plantation's main crop was rice. Whitney learned some of the land was not good for rice crops. But this land would grow large amounts of cotton. Even so, there was no easy way to clean so much cotton. A machine would make the job much faster.

Whitney wanted to tell his father about the new direction his life was taking. So he took out his pen and ink and began writing a letter. Whitney explained that he had "struck out a plan of a machine in my mind, which I communicated to Miller."[1]

Miller liked Whitney's idea. He even agreed to pay to build the machine if the idea worked. Miller gave Whitney a room in the basement to use as a workshop.

▲ **Whitney's original model was small enough to be operated by a hand crank.**

In this workshop, Whitney had to make the tools he would need to build the cotton gin. The term *gin* was short for *engine*.

Whitney got started. He built a small, experimental model of the machine in about ten days. Miller and Mrs. Greene were the only two people allowed into the workshop. In Whitney's letter, he told his father that the machine was a "profound secret."[2]

Whitney claimed his machine could be operated by a single person. He wrote, "One man will clean ten times as much cotton as he can in any other way before known."[3] The only cotton ginning machine available was a roller gin. It had been in use for centuries. It removed the seeds from long-staple cotton. This machine crushed the cottonseeds between **revolving** cylinders to remove them.

Although Whitney's design was a little different, he knew it would work. He constructed the cotton gin on a larger scale. He showed Miller the cylinder inside the gin's frame. It was made of wood. Rows of iron teeth covered the cylinder.

Whitney cranked the gin by hand. The cylinder rotated in one direction. The teeth pulled the seeded cotton from the hopper. The teeth then passed through a slotted grating. The cotton fiber was pulled through the slot. The seed was too large to pass through, so it remained behind. A clearer rotated in the opposite direction from the cylinder. The clearer brushed the cotton fiber from the cylinder's teeth.

Miller was amazed by Whitney's new machine. Whitney explained that larger gins would be built. Those would not be cranked by hand. Instead, they would be turned by waterwheels or horses.

Chapter 3

OBTAINING A PATENT

Whitney was excited about his new machine. In May 1793, he returned home to Connecticut to perfect the gin. Whitney told his father that people who knew of the invention expected it to make him rich. He continued, "I am now so sure of success that ten thousand dollars, if I saw the money counted out to me, would not tempt me to give up my right and **relinquish** the object."[4]

To make his fortune, Whitney knew he needed a patent. This license would give him alone the right to make and sell the cotton gin. Others would not be allowed to use his design to build machines of their own.

Whitney studied the 1793 Patent Act. He found out that he needed to send drawings to the secretary of state. He also had to send a written description and a model. On June 20, 1793, Whitney applied for a patent from Thomas Jefferson, the secretary of state. On October 15, 1793, Whitney mailed the descriptions to Jefferson. Whitney apologized for the four-month delay since filing the application.

Whitney was thrilled when he received a response from Jefferson. He took a deep breath as he opened the letter. It was dated November 16, 1793. Jefferson told Whitney that the only thing still missing was the model. Jefferson assured Whitney that the patent would be issued as soon as he received it. Whitney smiled as he read the end of Jefferson's note. Jefferson said he was interested in buying a cotton gin for his personal use!

By December 1793, Whitney had become frustrated with his model. It had been six months since he filed the patent application. He knew he needed to get the model to Jefferson.

ELI WHITNEY'S PATENT DRAWING

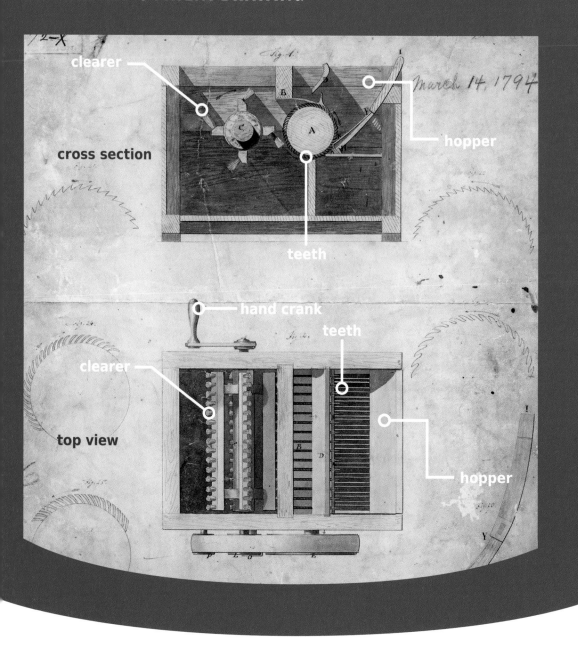

clearer

cross section

hopper

teeth

March 14, 1794

hand crank

teeth

clearer

top view

hopper

He spent many hours in his workshop. He experimented with different materials.

The cylinder was causing problems. The wood often split as he hammered the metal teeth into it. At first he wondered if the type of wood was causing the problem. Then he rethought his design. He realized he was hammering the metal teeth parallel to the wood's grain. So he tried something new. He hammered the teeth across the grain. It made a huge difference. This time, the toothed cylinder worked without splitting.

Whitney continued to perfect the design. By the spring of 1794, he had finished the working model. He submitted it to Jefferson. The patent was awarded on March 14, 1794.

Whitney formed a business partnership with Phineas Miller on June 21, 1794. They began operating under the name Miller & Whitney. After all, Miller had funded Whitney as he invented the gin. Miller had also paid for Whitney's manufacturing building in Connecticut.

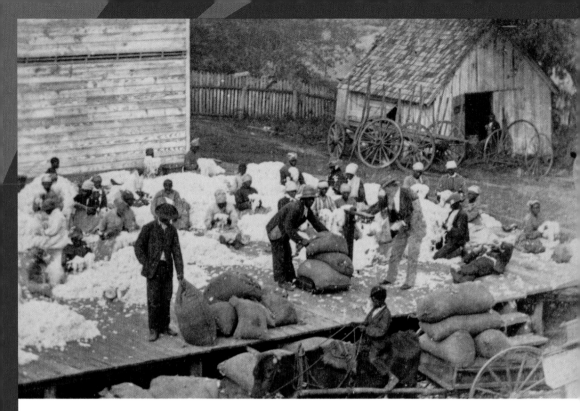

Chapter 4

BUSINESS STRUGGLES

Whitney felt confident. He loaded up his first shipment of the newly patented cotton gins. He set out from his workshop in Connecticut and headed for Mulberry Grove Plantation. Whitney arrived in May 1794. He delivered the gins to Miller. Whitney stayed in Georgia for three months. He knew there was much to be done to get the business up and running.

He helped Miller set up ginneries in Georgia and South Carolina. The partners chose waterwheels to install at their water-powered ginneries. They selected horses to power the animal-driven ginneries.

Miller & Whitney decided not to sell the cotton gins. Instead, they operated a service. Farmers brought cotton from their fields to the ginneries. This cotton included the green seeds. Miller & Whitney did the ginning. They cleaned out the seeds.

Miller & Whitney had a plan for making their fortune. They would charge farmers a significant portion of the ginned cotton as a fee. But farmers soon became angry. They didn't appreciate being charged such a high fee. So farmers began illegally building their own gins. Whitney couldn't believe it. The farmers were stealing his idea!

Miller & Whitney put a notice in several Georgia newspapers. It read, "Several attempts have been made, under the pretext of improvements on their machine, to trespass on their rights."[5] They reminded readers that Miller & Whitney was the only company allowed to sell a gin that used "teeth instead of rollers to draw the cotton from the seed, and a brush to clear the teeth."[6]

▲ **Most cotton gins were much larger than Whitney's original model.**

In March 1795, Whitney made a trip to New York for business. While there, he started feeling ill. He had a fever. He shivered and felt chilled. Whitney didn't think he could make the return trip home. So he stayed for three weeks until he was healthy enough to travel home.

Slaves operated cotton gins while plantation owners profited ▶ from their labor.

Whitney was still suffering chills when his boat arrived in Connecticut. Whitney felt his stomach drop as friends met his boat with the news. His workshop had burned the day before. All his cotton gins were gone. His documents were all burned. He was out of money. And he had no way to pay his debts.

Whitney soon began hearing rumors. **Textile** mills said his cotton gin produced poor-quality fiber. They claimed the cotton from his gin had small knots in it. Knots in cotton made production of yarn or fabric difficult. Whitney was furious. In 1796, he received a letter from Miller. "Everyone is afraid of the cotton," Miller wrote. "Not a purchaser in Savannah will pay full price for it."[7]

Whitney heard of another cotton gin being sold. He believed it violated his patent. It was called a saw gin. It was very similar to Whitney's gin. But it used fine-toothed saws instead of wire teeth. Miller & Whitney began to file **lawsuits** against the manufacturers that were copying their gin.

The two men spent the next few years buried in lawsuits. Their legal fees grew and grew. Much to their disappointment, they never made their fortune on cotton gins. Even so, the cotton gin had a huge impact. Plantation owners could now make more money than ever before on cotton.

◀ **Most of the cotton produced on American plantations went to textile mills in the United Kingdom.**

Chapter 5

IMPACT OF THE COTTON GIN

The steamboat captain stared at the river ahead of him. He had lost count of how many times he had been up and down this river. He was transporting a load of cotton to textile mills in New England. The year was 1860. New machines had been invented to spin and weave the cotton into fabric.

Textile mills had sprung up all over New England. The demand for the South's cotton had increased.

The steamboat captain had a plentiful supply of cotton to transport. Eli Whitney had invented the cotton gin at the end of the 1700s. Since then, the demand for cotton gins on southern plantations and farms had grown. Farmers began planting more acres of cotton. The cotton gin allowed them to separate seeds from cotton quickly. Cotton became more profitable. After 1800, the production of raw cotton had doubled every ten years. In fact, cotton made up 60 percent of the country's **exports** by 1860.

As the captain made these trips, he noticed more and more slave labor in the South. He had read that one in three southerners was a slave. There were now 15 states that allowed slavery. In 1790, there had been only eight. The U.S. Congress banned the import of slaves in 1808. But between 1790 and 1808, approximately 80,000 slaves were brought in from Africa. Many of these slaves worked on large cotton plantations. The cotton gin had lessened the time-consuming task of removing the seeds from cotton. But the cotton industry was growing. That meant plantation owners needed more slaves to pick the cotton.

The steamboat captain had heard the phrase Cotton Is King. Now, he understood it. He was making more money than he ever had. He was working constantly. New England textile mills were using 284 million pounds (128 million kg) of cotton a year. That was 67 percent of all cotton used by mills in the United States. So the captain would continue to travel up and down this river as long as King Cotton was in demand.

THINK ABOUT IT

- Did advancements in cotton-ginning technology benefit everyone? Why or why not?
- How might life on a southern farm have been different before and after getting a cotton gin?
- Suppose Miller & Whitney had sold the cotton gins rather than setting up a ginning service. How might their fortune have been different?

◀ Slaves endured horrible conditions on their way from Africa to North America.

GLOSSARY

clearer (KLEER-ur): A clearer is the set of rotating brushes that sweep the cotton fibers off the cotton gin's teeth. The clearer rotated in an opposite direction from the gin's cylinder.

exports (EX-ports): Exports are goods sent out of the country for sale. Cotton was one of the South's largest exports.

hopper (HOP-ur): A hopper is a container that stores some type of material. The cotton gin's hopper held the seeded cotton.

lawsuits (LAW-soots): Lawsuits are legal processes in which disagreements are decided in court. Whitney filed lawsuits against people who copied his cotton gin.

manufacture (man-yoo-FAK-shur): Manufacture means to turn raw materials into finished products, especially in a factory. Whitney built a factory to manufacture cotton gins.

patent (PAT-unt): A patent is a government license giving the right to sell an invention for a set amount of time. Whitney's patent gave him the right to make, use, and sell cotton gins for 14 years.

plantation (plan-TAY-shun): A plantation is a large farm for growing certain crops. Cotton and tobacco were some of the crops grown on a plantation.

relinquish (re-LIN-quish): Relinquish means to give something up. Whitney did not want to relinquish his idea for the cotton gin.

revolving (re-VOL-ving): Revolving means rotating or spinning. The clearer and the cylinder were revolving in opposite directions.

textile (TEX-tyl): A textile is a woven cloth or fabric. Textile mills produced fabric.

SOURCE NOTES

1. "Letter from Eli Whitney, Jr. to His Father regarding His Invention of the Cotton Gin, 11 September 1793." *Teaching American History in South Carolina.* Teaching American History in South Carolina Project, n.d. Web. 11 July 2016.

2. Ibid.

3. Ibid.

4. Ibid.

5. Angela Lakwete. *Inventing the Cotton Gin: Machine and Myth in Antebellum America.* Baltimore: Johns Hopkins University Press, 2003. Print. 60.

6. Ibid.

7. Ibid. 63.

TO LEARN MORE

Books

Colby, Jennifer. *Plants We Wear*. Ann Arbor, MI: Cherry Lake, 2014.

Garcia, Tracy J. *Eli Whitney*. New York: PowerKids Press, 2013.

Niver, Heather Moore. *Eli Whitney and the Industrial Revolution*. New York: PowerKids Press, 2016.

Web Sites

Visit our Web site for links about the invention of the cotton gin:

childsworld.com/links

Note to Parents, Teachers, and Librarians: We routinely verify our Web links to make sure they are safe and active sites. So encourage your readers to check them out!

INDEX